The One

The One:
Reaching the Lost
with the Love of Christ

Participant Book
978-1-7910-0031-8
978-1-7910-0032-5 *ePub*

Leader Guide
978-1-7910-0033-2
978-17910-0034-9 *ePub*

DVD
978-1-7910-0035-6

A Bible Study from Luke 15

the
o1e

reaching the lost with
the love of Christ

Jim and Jennifer Cowart

Abingdon Press | Nashville

THE ONE
REACHING THE LOST WITH THE LOVE OF CHRIST

Library of Congress Control Number: 2020936648

ISBN-13: 978-1-7910-0031-8

21 22 23 24 25 26 27 28 29 30—10 9 8 7 6 5 4 3 2 1

MANUFACTURED IN THE UNITED STATES OF AMERICA

To our kids, Alyssa, Josh, and Andrew,

who are passionate about life, Jesus,

and reaching the One.

CONTENTS

INTRODUCTION

He [Jesus] said to them, "Go into all the world and
preach the gospel to all creation."

(Mark 16:15 NIV)

"Who is your One?"

We were asked this question in a leadership develop-
ment meeting. Immediately we both said, "Jesus." That is
usually the correct church response. But it was wrong. So,
the question came again: "Who is your One?" We pointed
at each other, thinking maybe the questioner meant who
on earth is your person. OK, then, "Jen is my One; Jim is
my One," we said. Wrong again. Honestly, we didn't know
where this guy was going with the question. It was a little
frustrating. So we asked him to narrow it down for us.

He said, "What I want to know is, Who is the One person
in your life for whom your heart is breaking because they are
living far from God? Who is that One person you are praying
for and believing in faith for, so that he or she may come to
know and love Jesus?"

"Ah, that One. Yes, now we know who you mean."

In Luke 15, the Pharisees and religious teachers—who could be compared to church leaders today—are complaining because Jesus is hanging out with a rough crowd.

> ¹*Tax collectors and other notorious sinners often came to listen to Jesus teach.* ²*This made the Pharisees and teachers of religious law complain that he was associating with such sinful people— even eating with them!*
>
> *(Luke 15:1-2)*

In response to their murmurs, Jesus tells three very famous stories of lost things. First there is a lost sheep, which the good shepherd leaves his flock to find and rescue. Next, there is a precious coin that a simple woman searches carefully for until she finds it. Then there is the tale of the son who is lost. (Actually, this tale is about two sons.) This boy, often called the prodigal, has wandered far from home. His choices have disappointed his family, but upon his return he finds his dad is genuinely thrilled to welcome home that which has been lost—his boy.

The point Jesus is making is clear: God cares about what is lost. In fact, we see that the shepherd, the woman, and the dad go to great lengths to search for what is lost. Their search is passionate. It is diligent. And when they finally find what has been lost, there is celebration.

As this storytelling session begins, we see that the Pharisees and teachers are annoyed at the energy and time Jesus is pouring into tax collectors and notorious sinners. His association with these people, even having meals with them, becomes the topic of gossip and grumbling. This is important, because it is this attitude that triggers these parables in the first place. Somewhere along the way, these "church leaders" had become so professional in "doing church" that they lost sight of their purpose in the first place.

Through these stories, Jesus addresses the timeless truth that all people matter.

Let's make this personal. Who is your One? If one or more people don't immediately come to mind, then you may want to begin now to pray that God reveals to you those in need of his love. Perhaps it will be someone close to you—a long-time friend or family member. Or it could be that God brings brand new people into your life. For us, the One has been as close as family members and as random as the carryout guy at our grocery store. Isn't God fun like that?

Not long ago I (Jen) volunteered to take a six-year-old to her first piano lesson when her parents had other obligations. It was a fun experience for this mom of young adult kids. Because she was a little nervous, I thought it might help to distract her; so we made cookies. Then as we were headed to the lesson, I asked her questions to keep her mind occupied. After a little small talk, she took the lead and said, "Now, Mrs. Jen, let's talk about heaven." Of course, I was on board for that. So, I asked, "What do you think heaven is like?"

Her response came quickly: "Well first, you know, of course, in heaven Bibles are made out of rainbows."

"No, I didn't know that—interesting." After she shared a few more creative ideas, I asked, "Since heaven is so awesome, why do you think God leaves us here on earth? What do you think he wants us to do?"

As I watched this little cutie in the rearview mirror, I saw her facial expression intensify. Then she replied, "Mrs. Jen, you know this! We are here to help get people to heaven, so they can join us where we are already going."

I said to myself, *Wow, she really gets it!*

Our main objective as believers is to love God and love people in real and practical ways. And it just doesn't get more practical than helping them find the love and eternal security found in Christ.

After the Resurrection, Jesus sent his disciples to Galilee and told them to wait for him there. Upon seeing Christ, they began to worship, and then he spoke these words to them: "I have been given all authority in heaven and on earth. Therefore, go and make disciples of all the nations, baptizing them in the name of the Father and the Son and the Holy Spirit. Teach these new disciples to obey all the commands I have given you. And be sure of this: I am with you always, even to the end of the age" (Matthew 28:18-20).

This passage is known as the Great Commission. These are our marching orders as the people of God. We have been tasked with sharing the love and message of Christ with those who don't know him. And we mean to share him, we really do. But then we get busy. Even in the church, we get busy doing churchy stuff. Before we know it, we are so busy with programs, studies, and services that we take our eyes off those who are lost and put them squarely on those who are already found—or even worse, on ourselves. Now, those who have been found need care and discipleship, but we have to find the balance of caring for those in the family while inviting others to join it.

We both have always been passionate about reaching people for Christ. Evangelism is at the core of who we are and how we do ministry. But after being asked "Who is your One?" in such a pointed way, we realized that we were not as intentional as a church family or as individuals as we had been at one time. The balance was off. We didn't mean to drift, but we had. Without realizing it, we had become so occupied with the care and discipleship of all the believers in our church that we were neglecting the work of reaching out to those in our community who had not yet found

God relevant in their lives: the lost. As a body of believers, we had to wrestle with how to put Luke 15 and the Great Commission into practice in new and fresh ways.

So, our team got to work reintroducing a culture of invitation and passion for the lost in our local setting. Through a four-week sermon series and small group sessions on Luke 15, we cast a vision and invited people to look for new and creative ways to reach those in their lives who did not have a relationship with Jesus. As part of that emphasis, we invited our people to write the first names of people in their lives who did not have a relationship with Jesus on the back of simple cards and pin them on the altar each week. We prayed for their Ones to have open hearts, and for church members to have courage to invite their Ones to church. Over 4,200 names were listed—and a surprising number of those cards simply said "Me." As a result of that four-week emphasis, our first-time worship attendance skyrocketed, which gave us the privilege of sharing Christ with new people. Best of all, we began to see more and more people accepting Christ. This book and the accompanying study materials are an outgrowth of that effort and are intended to help you and your church cultivate a passion for reaching people for Christ in your own local setting.

Together we will explore Luke 15, a chapter dedicated to finding what is lost. Through the stories of the lost sheep, coin, and child, Jesus reveals the heart of our heavenly Father. He is a God who grieves over those who are far from him—and those who have strayed.

This book will help you explore at a personal level, as a group, and corporately as a local church how you, too, can rekindle and recommit to living out the Great Commission. We hope in the coming days you will become even more passionate about the One, or Ones, in your own lives. As a caution, remember that this is not a study about taking people on as a project—yuck, no one wants that. It's about becoming intentional in sharing the love and message of Jesus. It may help to think of the title of this study, *The One*, as more of a question than a statement. Within your congregation, we hope it becomes more of a purpose statement and culture than a one-off church program or study.

Who is your One? Whom do you know who needs Jesus?

So, Who is your One? Whom do you know who needs Jesus? Who can you pray for, invite, and pursue in much the same way a parent would pursue a lost child? One of our favorite definitions of evangelism is "one beggar helping another beggar find bread."[1] We who follow Christ are simply beggars who have found a plentiful food source. So, let's share what we have found!

Or, perhaps what is lost is you. You may be the One who needs to be found. If that's the case, then there's great news: this book is meant for you too! Jesus wants to meet you right where you are. You are loved. You are chosen. You are the One for whom he would search high and low to reach. Wherever you are in your journey, welcome to *The One*! We're glad you're along for this exciting ride as we explore God's deep love for each and every One of us!

Jim and Jen

THE THREE PARABLES OF LUKE 15

Parable of the Lost Sheep

[4]*"If a man has a hundred sheep and one of them gets lost, what will he do? Won't he leave the ninety-nine others in the wilderness and go to search for the one that is lost until he finds it? [5]And when he has found it, he will joyfully carry it home on his shoulders. [6]When he arrives, he will call together his friends and neighbors, saying, 'Rejoice with me because I have found my lost sheep.' [7]In the same way, there is more joy in heaven over one lost sinner who repents and returns to God than over ninety-nine others who are righteous and haven't strayed away!"*

(Luke 15:4-7)

Parable of the Lost Coin

8"Or suppose a woman has ten silver coins and loses one. Won't she light a lamp and sweep the entire house and search carefully until she finds it? 9And when she finds it, she will call in her friends and neighbors and say, 'Rejoice with me because I have found my lost coin.' 10In the same way, there is joy in the presence of God's angels when even one sinner repents."

(Luke 15:8-10)

Parable of the Lost Son

¹¹*To illustrate the point further, Jesus told them this story: "A man had two sons.* ¹²*The younger son told his father, 'I want my share of your estate now before you die.' So his father agreed to divide his wealth between his sons.*

¹³*"A few days later this younger son packed all his belongings and moved to a distant land, and there he wasted all his money in wild living.* ¹⁴*About the time his money ran out, a great famine swept over the land, and he began to starve.* ¹⁵*He persuaded a local farmer to hire him, and the man sent him into his fields to feed the pigs.* ¹⁶*The young man became so hungry that even the pods he was feeding the pigs looked good to him. But no one gave him anything.*

¹⁷*"When he finally came to his senses, he said to himself, 'At home even the hired servants have food enough to spare, and here I am dying of hunger!* ¹⁸*I will go home to my father and say, "Father, I have sinned against both heaven and you,* ¹⁹*and I am no longer worthy of being called your son. Please take me on as a hired servant."'*

²⁰*"So he returned home to his father. And while he was still a long way off, his father saw him coming. Filled with love and compassion, he ran to his son, embraced him, and kissed him.* ²¹*His son said to him, 'Father, I have sinned against both heaven and you, and I am no longer worthy of being called your son.'*

22"But his father said to the servants, 'Quick! Bring the finest robe in the house and put it on him. Get a ring for his finger and sandals for his feet. 23And kill the calf we have been fattening. We must celebrate with a feast, 24for this son of mine was dead and has now returned to life. He was lost, but now he is found.' So the party began.

25"Meanwhile, the older son was in the fields working. When he returned home, he heard music and dancing in the house, 26and he asked one of the servants what was going on. 27'Your brother is back,' he was told, 'and your father has killed the fattened calf. We are celebrating because of his safe return.'

28"The older brother was angry and wouldn't go in. His father came out and begged him, 29but he replied, 'All these years I've slaved for you and never once refused to do a single thing you told me to. And in all that time you never gave me even one young goat for a feast with my friends. 30Yet when this son of yours comes back after squandering your money on prostitutes, you celebrate by killing the fattened calf!'

31"His father said to him, 'Look, dear son, you have always stayed by me, and everything I have is yours. 32We had to celebrate this happy day. For your brother was dead and has come back to life! He was lost, but now he is found!'"

(Luke 15:11-32)

YOU ARE THE ONE

Luke 19:1-9

JEN

"For God so loved the world that he gave his one and only Son, that whoever believes in him shall not perish but have eternal life."

(John 3:16 NIV)

Do you know what an Amber Alert is? It's an emergency response system that goes out through multiple media sources when a child is missing. When we hear the beeping and the alert crosses the screen, our hearts always skip a beat, because in that moment we know that somewhere in the world there is a parent who has just become consumed with only one mission in life. Everything else fades away and only one thing remains: finding what is lost! Whatever it takes, whoever needs to get involved, whatever the cost may be, that parent has to find his or her child.

When our daughter, Alyssa, was about four months old, I laid her down on a blanket in our den and went to get her favorite toy in the next room. When I returned less than a minute later, the blanket was empty. She was gone. I began to panic. No one else was in the house. Frantically, I began to think, *What could possibly have happened? Where is she?*

Could someone have taken her? In a matter of seconds, I went from the joy of spending the morning with my newborn into full-blown emergency mode. I ran from room to room looking for her. No sign of her anywhere. So, I grabbed the phone to call Jim, and through tears I began to tell him what had happened. Then, I heard a slight noise.

It was a happy coo really. I dropped the phone and began to follow the sound. She was under a cloth-covered table, several yards away from where I had laid her—completely out of sight! Apparently, she had chosen that moment while I was in the kitchen to learn to roll. And roll she did! Not once, but apparently several times, in order to end up as far away from her blanket as she had. (She's always been a kid to do things to the extreme.)

She was perfectly safe, but those few minutes of panic remain with me to this day. The idea of my precious child being lost, separated from me, left a mark on me I will never forget. In those moments I was desperate. My whole world was narrowed to just one thing: find my lost child!

As I read through Luke 15, I relive those moments. I feel the passion I had for Alyssa, and I imagine Jesus speaking to the crowd. As He tells these three famous parables, He is wanting to convey to everyone assembled that those who are lost are precious. From the perspective of a parent, I understand this, but from the perspective of a child, it's harder to grasp. Jesus is illustrating the passion God feels for us.

Read these verses again and notice the love that is illustrated:

THE SHEEP:

> *"There is more joy in heaven over one lost sinner*
> *who repents and returns to God than over ninety-*

nine others who are righteous and haven't strayed away!"

(Luke 15:7)

THE COIN:

"When she finds it, she will call in her friends and neighbors and say, 'Rejoice with me because I have found my lost coin.'"

(Luke 15:9)

THE SON:

"While he was still a long way off, his father saw him coming. Filled with love and compassion, he ran to his son, embraced him, and kissed him."

(Luke 15:20)

These verses show us that Jesus is passionate about lost things. In fact, in Luke 19:10 (NKJV) we read, "The Son of Man has come to seek and to save that which was lost." This is a well-known verse, but do you know the context in which we find it? It's the closing verse of a unique encounter that Jesus has with a tax collector named Zacchaeus.

Zacchaeus Meets Jesus

If this story is familiar, try to read it in a fresh way today. First, imagine the setting, the city of Jericho. It's hot. The hills beyond the palms are barren, but there is life in town because the teacher everyone has been talking about is coming through. Jesus, the healer, the controversial leader, has come to town, and the crowds have gathered. Now, put yourself into the story, imagining that you are Zacchaeus. You want to get to Jesus. But, like at a political rally or concert, the crowd is a dense mass of humanity, and getting a front-row seat seems impossible. So, you have a crazy idea: I'll climb this tree and get a balcony seat for the show. Note what you feel as you read the story:

> ¹*Jesus entered Jericho and was passing through.*
> ²*A man was there by the name of Zacchaeus; he was a chief tax collector and was wealthy.* ³*He wanted to see who Jesus was, but because he was short he could not see over the crowd.* ⁴*So he ran ahead and climbed a sycamore-fig tree to see him, since Jesus was coming that way.*
>
> ⁵*When Jesus reached the spot, he looked up and said to him, "Zacchaeus, come down immediately. I must stay at your house today."* ⁶*So he came down at once and welcomed him gladly.*
>
> ⁷*All the people saw this and began to mutter, "He has gone to be the guest of a sinner."*
>
> ⁸*But Zacchaeus stood up and said to the Lord, "Look, Lord! Here and now I give half of my possessions to the poor, and if I have cheated anybody out of anything, I will pay back four times the amount."*
>
> ⁹*Jesus said to him, "Today salvation has come to this house, because this man, too, is a son of Abraham.* ¹⁰***For the Son of Man came to seek and to save the lost.****"*
>
> *(Luke 19:1-10 NIV, emphasis added)*

What did you feel as you read the story? Could you relate to Zacchaeus? Could you feel the surprise, the embarrassment, and the awkwardness as the man leading the parade looked into your eyes and called you by name? What did you feel as you were singled out in the crowd and then allowed to host Jesus in your home? What did you feel as you realized that Jesus knows your name, and he called to you today?

***What did you feel as you realized
that Jesus knows your name,
and he called to you today?***

Jim and I grew up as Sunday school kids, attending vacation Bible school and singing the song of the wee little man who climbed up in the sycamore tree. So this story is familiar to us. We have heard many sermons centered around how shocking it was that Jesus noticed, called down, and then ate with a man known as a cheat in the community. We know the history: Jewish tax collectors for the Roman government were not popular figures. Their profession centered around taking advantage of those in the community. Zacchaeus had hurt many people. He had done things he was not proud of and surely stood in need of forgiveness from many. He was a sinner living far from God. But Jesus called his name. Zacchaeus did not deserve the attention and grace shown to him. But, then again, neither do we. It's easy to imagine the outrage of the crowd, but what was Zacchaeus feeling? Could he even imagine that someone so pure, so loving, would want to spend time with him?

Now, remember that for today you are the One in the tree. Jesus is calling your name.

Personalizing God's Promises

*But God demonstrates his own love for us in this:
While we were still sinners, Christ died for us.*
(Romans 5:8 NIV)

5

In the following chapters, we are going to concentrate on teaming up with God to reach those who are living far from God. We'll do a deep dive into how to reach the Ones in your life. But for now, we want to focus on the fact that at one time, maybe even currently, that One is you. You are the One in the tree to whom Jesus says, "I see you, and I love you!"

Before we become passionate about sharing Christ with others, we have to become secure in the fact that he first loved us. We have to personalize his promises and come to a heartfelt understanding that we are God's dearly loved children.

Jim and I have been in ministry since we were teenagers. Reading, meditating on, and studying Scripture is part of how we do life. But understanding and embracing how that applies to me personally was a challenge for many years. "For God so loved the world that he gave his one and only Son" (John 3:16 NIV). OK, I understand that. For God so loved Jim, and my kids, and my staff—of course, *they're* all precious. Surely this applies to them.

But *me*? I am the One? That's harder for me to grasp. I mean, maybe I could be part of the crowd, maybe even a disciple traveling with Jesus in Jericho, but the One? That has been a more challenging concept for me to accept. Is it hard for you?

One of our dear friends is a Maasai warrior in Kenya. He is also a precious man of God. When we see him, he often greets us with the traditional African greeting of *"I see you."* Spoken with his beautiful accent, it is a verbal declaration of more than acute eyesight. It is his warm way of saying, *I know you, I care about you, I love you.* Likewise, when Jesus calls to Zacchaeus, he is saying, "I see you. I value you. Let's spend time together. You are important."

In Luke 15 we read, "Tax collectors and other notorious sinners often came to listen to Jesus teach. This made the Pharisees and teachers of religious law complain that he was associating with such sinful people—even eating with them!" (vv. 1-2). These first two verses are powerful. If we pass over them too quickly and move directly to the parables, we may miss the fact that Jesus welcomed messy people. Tax collectors like Zacchaeus, along with other notorious sinners like me and probably like you, often spent time listening to Jesus share life-giving truths. Well, I don't know if our sins are notorious, but who knows, in heaven they just may be.

As I read these three parables in Luke 15, at times I relate to the woman searching for the coin or the sheep who has wandered away or the prodigal son—sometimes even the self-righteous older brother. In my finer moments, I feel the love of the Father welcoming and rejoicing over One who has been lost. But perhaps most of all, I can relate to these sinners in the story of Zacchaeus who are unworthy to even be there with Jesus. Yet Jesus didn't just teach them; he spent time with them. Luke gets specific when he tells us that, as with Zacchaeus, Jesus even ate with them.

A meal during this time period was not fast-food pickup. It was a social event, usually hours long. So, when the Scripture mentions that Jesus took the time to eat with these people who were not considered holy by the Pharisees' standards, he was spending quality time with them. He cared about their stories. Jesus wanted to know them, and He wanted them to know him. He didn't just allow them to listen in as he instructed the more righteous members of the community. They weren't his pet projects. He spent time with them and considered them friends. What was his motivation here? Love. Simply put, he wanted them to experience his love and develop a real and intimate relationship with them.

Jesus Knows Your Name

May you be able to feel and understand, as all God's children should, how long, how wide, how deep, and how high his love really is; and to experience this love for yourselves, though it is so great that you will never see the end of it or fully know or understand it. And so at last you will be filled up with God himself.

(Ephesians 3:18 TLB)

I went to church camps growing up. I knew the Bible pretty well, and overall I was a well-behaved adolescent. So, it came as a shock to me when one of the older kids in my youth group came to me on a retreat and shared with me that she wanted me to know Jesus. I was insulted. I had been through confirmation. I had been baptized. I went to Sunday school. What else did she want from me?

She went on to share that she was afraid I only knew of God and his Son, but that I did not know Christ personally—that I had not yet developed a personal relationship with him. In retrospect, it was precious, but at the time, I was ticked. Who did she think she was?

In my anger—and conviction—I went and sat alone a few minutes, and during that time God really spoke to me. She was right. I had not yet embraced a personal relationship with Jesus. All of the knowledge and "good" living was not bringing me peace and joy. I had not yet found the intimacy of knowing Jesus for myself. It was in those moments that I accepted more than forgiveness of my sins and embraced the Son of God in a more intimate way. I had been in the church since birth, but on that day, through this girl's gentle confrontation, I began a relationship with Christ. I began to understand a truth that still overwhelms me to this day—I am the One!

It was probably difficult for the notorious sinners and common people who gathered about Jesus to understand that this great teacher, the One who performed the miracles, could love them. And, surely, it was hard for the tax collector of Jericho, Zacchaeus. What about for you? Is it hard for you to understand that John 3:16 is written especially for you? For God so loved (insert your name here) that Jesus came and suffered, died, and was resurrected.

It's an overwhelming, life-changing, heart-melting truth. And it applies to you!

Understanding that we are the One is a deep and precious truth. Like Zacchaeus, Jesus knows your name. Don't miss that! *Jesus knows you.* You are the lost sheep that he would leave the ninety-nine to search for. You are the coin of great value that he would tear apart the house to find. And you are the child that he runs to embrace.

If you have never made a decision to follow Jesus as your Lord and are ready to do that, or if you would like to recommit your life to him today, pray something like this:

> *Dear God, thank you for your love. Please forgive me for rejecting your ways and choosing to live by my own standards. I receive Jesus as my Lord and Savior and want to begin today to live for you. Help me to know you and follow you. Amen.*

If this is your first time praying that prayer, or if you are praying it as a recommitment to Christ, congratulations and welcome (or welcome back) to the family! You are forgiven. Your sins are washed away, and Jesus will continue to draw you to himself. Now, you will need a church family to encourage and guide you. Having others who also are seeking to live in a way that pleases God will help you grow and hold you accountable. It's a beautiful thing to be the One Jesus loves!

FOR INSPIRATION

Wesley's Story

Growing up in a family that professed Christianity but really had nothing to do with Jesus left me with little interest in God. Watching hypocrisy among some of the believers I did know drove me further and further from Christ. In fact, as I went off to college, I had decided I was doing just fine without him. Wanting to make friends on this new mega-campus, I wandered into a Christian gathering for a game night. When one of the leaders came up to greet me, I quickly said, "I am just here to enjoy the game night; I'm not interested in the whole Jesus thing." It did not faze this guy! He responded by saying, "That's cool, man, we don't have to talk about Jesus. You're tall. Do you play basketball?"

We played ball a few times and a friendship developed. This guy cared about me. He didn't shove his faith down my throat but simply was present in my life, ready to share when I was ready. I think he knew I would come around. It showed in how he pursued me. Something he still does to this day. This man, now a dear friend, has loved me with no agenda but to know me and have me come to know his Savior.

Through his friendship and prayers, I eventually became interested in Christianity. But I wrestled with sin and anxiety more than I ever had. During my struggles, he was there to patiently guide me. After three years of struggling and searching, I accepted Jesus as Lord and decided to be baptized. I have come to know that Jesus loves me deeply. He has pursued me my whole life, and through this precious friendship, I came to understand that. A relationship that started with me abrasively telling this man that I wanted nothing to do with the most important truth I could ever hear blossomed into me not only finally believing that truth but also letting it guide my daily life. Without this passionate Christ-follower, I would not have married my wife, who is a devoted follower of Jesus. I would not have found a passion for student ministry, and I don't know where I would be today.

I am so thankful for my friend's passion and patience as he sought to share Christ with me. He saw me as the One, and I am forever grateful. Often, I hearken back to how Jesus pursued me through another person. I am now in a position to pursue other people in much the same way through a high school boys ministry that often has young men who are struggling with crippling doubts much in the same way I was. When in the position to share the gospel, or to help someone, I always remind myself of a quote often attributed to Theodore Roosevelt: "no one cares how much you know, until they know how much you care." In order for me to bring people to Jesus, I first have to care about people, even though they may reject me. And if they reject me, maybe what they need in that moment is not a sermon but just someone to play basketball with.

I am the One,
Wesley

FOR MEMORIZATION

Believe in the Lord Jesus, and you will be saved.
(Acts 16:31 NIV)

FOR REFLECTION

- What emotions do you experience as you think about the God of the universe calling your name?
- Who has been a significant part of your faith journey?
- When did you come to realize that you were the One?
- Who might the "tax collectors and other notorious sinners" be in our culture today?
- How would your church respond if these sinners came through the doors of your church? How would you respond?
- Begin today to make a list of the Ones in your life.

THE SHEEP

Luke 15:1-7

JIM

"For God did not send His Son into the world to condemn the world, but that the world through Him might be saved."

(John 3:17 NKJV)

Who is your One?

That's the question we're continuing to ask ourselves as we look deeper into the lost and found stories Jesus tells in Luke 15. Of course, that question can mean many things, but for our purposes it means, Who is the One person in your life right now who is lost, hurting, or far from God? Who are you brokenhearted over because that person you care about is not walking close to Jesus?

Now, if I am being honest, sometimes my answer to that question is no one. And that's a problem. If you're honest, you might answer that same way at times. If we aren't intentional, we can go for weeks, months, or even years without really seeking to share Christ with others. And that is a big problem! It means we are not living into the most important directive Jesus ever gave us. Why would that happen?

Well, sometimes we just get busy—or at least distracted. Our agendas tend to overshadow the marching orders of our Savior, Jesus. We know the Great Commandment. We can recite the Great Commission. Our directions are clear— love God, love people, and share God with those who don't yet know him—but life gets busy. And friend, God doesn't want any of us distracted, unproductive, or sitting on the sidelines. As we've already seen, Jesus has told us clearly what our mission on earth is. It's the same one he had, and it's stated clearly in Luke 19: "For the Son of Man came to seek and save those who are lost" (Luke 19:10).

There's another reason we may not be able to identify the One in our life. It's because we're it! We are the One. As Jen said in chapter 1, sometimes we are the One who is lost or hurting, the One who is living far from God. If that's been your situation, then I hope you chose to give or recommit your life to God as you read the previous chapter. You are the One! And so is every person you will ever meet. Now, let's set the stage for the first of the three parables in Luke 15.

Sometimes we are the One who is lost or hurting, the One who is living far from God.

We Are Like Sheep

The first story Jesus shares with the crowd is all about livestock. Sheep, to be specific. So let's think about those little creatures for a moment. They are cute and cuddly, but among the members of the animal kingdom, they are not the sharpest tools in the shed, or at least they don't appear that way. They tend to wander off and get themselves into trouble. They are virtually defenseless without the care of their shepherd. Yet these particular animals are mentioned many times in the Bible and often are used as a metaphor for me and you. We are God's wandering, not-always-so-bright sheep who live in need of a shepherd. As the prophet Isaiah wrote,

> *All of us, like sheep, have strayed away.*
> *We have left God's paths to follow our own.*
> *(Isaiah 53:6a)*

Have you been to a circus lately? There are lions and tigers and bears, but I've never seen sheep called into the center ring. There are no circus acts featuring courageous little lambs. As far as I know, there are no seeing-eye sheep or attack sheep, and they don't get featured in movies as the hero. Just try to imagine Lassie as a sheep. "What is it, girl? Timmy has fallen into an abandoned well—again? Lead the way! Baaaaaaaa!"

Even the term *sheepish* has a negative connotation. I mean, if someone is known as being "sheepish," that's usually not meant as a compliment. It portrays someone who is shy, bashful, perhaps even cowardly. And sheep aren't exactly what we're looking for on dating profiles: "Single who loves long walks on the beach, getting caught in the rain, and being timid, afraid, and awkward around other human beings." Not too appealing, is it?

In short, sheep just aren't known for their intelligence or bravery. They need protection, care, and direction. They need a leader. That's where the shepherd comes in. I think we're referred to as sheep in the Bible because, like these woolly, four-legged creatures, we're kind of cute but have a tendency to wander off and get into trouble. Hey, if the wool fits, we've gotta wear it!

The Sheep and the Goats

We may be sheep, but we shouldn't be discouraged. Being called a biblical, metaphorical sheep sure beats being called a biblical, metaphorical goat! In Matthew 25 Jesus describes a chilling scene that's coming in the future judgment of the world.

> [31]*"But when the Son of Man comes in his glory, and all the angels with him, then he will sit upon his glorious throne. [32]All the nations will be gathered in his presence, and he will separate the people as a shepherd separates the sheep from the goats. [33]He will place the sheep at his right hand and the goats at his left.*
>
> [34]*"Then the King will say to those on his right, 'Come, you who are blessed by my Father, inherit the Kingdom prepared for you from the creation of the world. [35]For I was hungry, and you fed me. I was thirsty, and you gave me a drink. I was a stranger, and you invited me into your home. [36]I was naked, and you gave me clothing. I was sick, and you cared for me. I was in prison, and you visited me.'*
>
> [37]*"Then these righteous ones will reply, 'Lord, when did we ever see you hungry and feed you? Or thirsty and give you something to drink? [38]Or a stranger and show you hospitality? Or naked and give you clothing? [39]When did we ever see you sick or in prison and visit you?'*
>
> [40]*"And the King will say, 'I tell you the truth, when you did it to one of the least of these my brothers and sisters, you were doing it to me!'*

*[41]"Then the King will turn to those on the left
and say, 'Away with you, you cursed ones, into
the eternal fire prepared for the devil and his
demons. [42]For I was hungry, and you didn't feed
me. I was thirsty, and you didn't give me a drink.
[43]I was a stranger, and you didn't invite me into
your home. I was naked, and you didn't give me
clothing. I was sick and in prison, and you didn't
visit me.'*

*[44]"Then they will reply, 'Lord, when did we ever
see you hungry or thirsty or a stranger or naked or
sick or in prison, and not help you?'*

*[45]"And he will answer, 'I tell you the truth, when
you refused to help the least of these my brothers
and sisters, you were refusing to help me.'*

*[46]"And they will go away into eternal punishment,
but the righteous will go into eternal life."*
(Matthew 25:31-46)

What a powerful illustration! This is a passage to which we should pay attention! It is a call to action.

Jesus explains here that when he returns, he will separate the nations as a shepherd separates the sheep from the goats.

That's pretty interesting. Sometimes we don't think about nations in heaven or in the new earth, but it seems that God continues to organize us in nations and cities even in his future Kingdom and the world to come. God will create a new heaven and a new earth. (Hey, this one is broken, so one day God will create a new one.) Often we get our idea of heaven from cartoons—with us floating around with little wings, playing harps from cloud to cloud. That sounds terrible to me! How boring! No, one day God will bring an end to this broken world and create a brand-new one where Jesus sits on the throne. It's going to be awesome!

> ¹*Then I saw "a new heaven and a new earth," for the first heaven and the first earth had passed away, and there was no longer any sea. ²I saw the Holy City, the new Jerusalem, coming down out of heaven from God, prepared as a bride beautifully dressed for her husband.*
>
> *(Revelation 21:1-2 NIV)*

Though Scripture doesn't say, perhaps we first will experience what we see described in Matthew 25. Here's how this scene of the sheep and the goats plays out in my imagination. Jesus is sitting on his throne, and the nations are gathered before him. It is the biggest crowd ever gathered, because this crowd comprises literally everyone in history! Everyone is here! But there's no pushing or shoving. Even though there are people as far as the eye can see, everyone can see and hear the One who sits on the throne, Jesus. The flags of each nation are stirring in the gentle breeze.

Some of the people under the Chinese flag wave to the Jamaicans standing nearby under their flag. People of the Congo are talking casually to the Australians, while everyone waits for the King to call them to order. It's a little like the presentation of the national teams during the Olympic Games, only much bigger and grander.

Somehow, without even speaking, King Jesus begins to reorganize the masses standing before him. At a silent signal, the tide of humanity moves slowly but steadily toward the throne like a wave washing up on the shore. As the massive crowd nears the throne, nations are mingled together and everyone—everyone—looks Jesus in the eye. Every person in history stands momentarily before that brilliant, shining throne. Without a word, the King, the Seer of Hearts, signals for each person to assemble either to his right side or his left side. Without a word, the nations begin to disperse to either side of Jesus. Some Austrians move to his right and some to his left. Some Zambians look Jesus in the eye and move left while others move right. The process continues with every nation until every human being finds himself or herself in a huge, blended crowd of all nationalities. All people from all the nations, tribes, and empires that have ever existed are now divided into just two groups: those standing on the King's right hand and those standing on his left.

The people on his right are called sheep. The ones on his left are the goats. Then both groups are presented with the same list of actions they did or did not do on behalf of Jesus.

To Jesus's right are the sheep who acted in love:

I was hungry, and you fed me.
I was thirsty, and you gave me a drink.
I was a stranger, and you invited me into your home.
I was naked, and you gave me clothing.
I was sick, and you cared for me.
I was in prison, and you visited me.

However, to the goats on his left, Jesus says:

I was hungry, and you didn't feed me.
I was thirsty, and you didn't give me a drink.
I was a stranger, and you didn't invite me into
your home.
I was naked, and you didn't give me clothing.
I was sick and in prison, and you didn't visit me.

Jesus welcomes the sheep into his Kingdom, but the goats are sent to the "eternal fire prepared for the devil and his angels" (Matthew 25:41 NIV).

It's interesting, and frightening, that both the people categorized as sheep and the ones categorized as goats have similar answers when Jesus speaks to them. Both ask the question, When? When did we help you or fail to help you? (vv. 37-39, 44). Jesus replies, "Whatever you did for one of the least of these brothers and sisters of mine, you did for me" (v. 40 NIV).

The story of the sheep and goats is both terrifying and heartbreaking. Did their works save the sheep? No. Ephesians 2:8-9 (NIV) says that "it is by grace you have been saved, through faith—and this is not from yourselves, it is the gift of God—not by works, so that no one can boast." But our works are evidence of our faith. James is clear in pointing out that a faith that has no works is not a vital faith at all: "Faith by itself, if it is not accompanied by action, is dead....A person is considered righteous by what they do and not by faith alone" (2:17, 24 NIV).

Whether sincere or not, the goats miss a real relationship with Jesus, which results in missing eternal life in heaven. Those are serious consequences. Sometimes people forget that being a follower of Jesus is not just about our beliefs or intentions. It's true that our works do not save us, but faith is also about putting correct beliefs into action. As James goes on to say, "As the body without the spirit is dead, so faith without deeds is dead" (2:26 NIV).

Jesus wants us to put our faith into action. We've got to walk the walk as well as talk the talk.

Dead faith does us no good! That's just stale, crusty religion. Jesus wants us to put our faith into action. We've got to walk the walk as well as talk the talk. A primary way we do that is by reaching out to those who are far from God and developing real relationships with them so that we might have the privilege of sharing Christ with them.

Think about it: in this story, there's only one thing that appears to separate the sheep from the goats—action! The sheep helped Jesus. How? By helping those Jesus called "the least of these." The goats, on the other hand, didn't help Jesus. Why? They did not care enough to get involved in helping others.

The expression "the least of these brothers and sisters" says a lot about the heart of Jesus. His mission on earth was to seek and to save those who were lost. Like the shepherd whose sheep have gone astray, Jesus is the Shepherd who seeks to bring them home. God loves all people, and he wants all people to be on his right side, the sheep side, at the final judgment.

Found People Find People

John 3:16 is probably the most famous verse in the Bible. It says, "For God so loved the world that He gave His only begotten Son, that whoever believes in Him should not perish but have everlasting life" (John 3:16 NKJV). But don't overlook what comes next: "For God did not send His Son into the world to condemn the world, but that the world through Him *might be saved*" (John 3:17 NKJV, emphasis added).

Lost people are important. God loves his sheep, but not only the sheep in his flock called the church. He also loves the sheep who are still out there, lost. He loves the One who has wandered away. He loves the One who doesn't even know he or she is lost. And he wants us to love them, too, and go find them!

In what is called the Great Commission, Jesus says, "Therefore, go and make disciples of all the nations, baptizing them in the name of the Father and the Son and the Holy Spirit. Teach these new disciples to obey all the commands I have given you. And be sure of this: I am with you always, even to the end of the age" (Matthew 28:19-20). Jesus is commissioning us, sending us out to carry on his mission to seek and save the lost.

Our church has a little saying that helps us remember to do the Great Commission, and it goes like this: "Found People Find People." If you've been found, then it's time for you to go out and find someone else who is lost. The Good Shepherd sends out his sheep to help find the lost Ones. This is not a task delegated to pastors or missionaries. This is a task for all of us sheep who follow Jesus. Why do we do this? Because when a person finds Christ, he or she finds new life—life that John 10:10 describes as abundant!

My friend Lee is one of the best inviters in our church. I think she feels this sense of urgency and concern for others because she remembers what it feels like to be a lost sheep. She lives with a passion for the One because she remembers so well the days where she was the One. She really lives out "Found People Find People." She knows that the goal is to be a sheep that is safely traveling beside its shepherd. (You'll find Lee's story at the end of this chapter.)

Job Descriptions for Sheep and Shepherd

The Shepherd loves his sheep. He does not care that the sheep can't do tricks. He doesn't expect them to fetch or protect his home. The Shepherd knows exactly the nature, abilities, and limitations of sheep—and he loves us anyway. He just expects sheep to be sheep and to follow the Shepherd.

John 10 is another place in the Bible where the sheep metaphor is used. Here Jesus calls himself the Good Shepherd and goes on to explain some of the job descriptions for both sheep and the shepherd.

Sheep Know the Shepherd's Voice

In John 10:5, we learn that the sheep know the shepherd's voice and won't follow a stranger. I saw an interesting video clip that shows a good shepherd interacting with his sheep. Here's the scene: A group of students is visiting a farm. A herd of sheep is grazing peacefully in the background, and several students are given the task of calling the sheep to try to get them to come to them. They feel silly but give it a shot. The sheep never stop grazing. After several failed attempts, the farmer steps forward and calls out. Within seconds the sheep recognize the farmer's voice and enthusiastically run to him from the farthest ends of the pasture. It's such a dramatic success after the students' failure that they are amazed and burst into cheers. It really is a powerful visual. There are no magic words. The sheep just recognize the voice of their shepherd. As we follow Jesus closely, we become more and more familiar with his voice and learn that he is a shepherd to be trusted. We can feel safe in running to him.

The Shepherd Is the Gate

In John 10:7, Jesus says that he is the gate for the sheep. Some commentators flesh this out a bit, explaining that when a shepherd was looking for fresh grazing land with his sheep, he or she might roam far from home and away from the normal corral. Out in the wilds, there would inevitably come times when rounding the sheep up for safety or care would be necessary. A cave or narrow canyon might do nicely for this, and the shepherd would then sleep in front of the opening of the improvised sheep enclosure, literally becoming the "gate" or "door" to the sheep. Perhaps you've heard the phrase "Over my dead body!" This seems to be the sweet sentiment Jesus uses to describe his love and dedication to his flock. We see Jesus put this very thing into action at the cross where he lays down his life for us.

The Shepherd Is Not a Hired Hand

Jesus calls himself the Good Shepherd and contrasts this role with that of a hired hand. When the going gets tough—in this case, a wolf attack—the hired hand might say, "I'm not getting paid enough for this! These stupid sheep aren't mine. I'm out of here!" But the Good Shepherd is different. The Good Shepherd lays down his life for his sheep. He will fight wolf and lion and bear to the death to protect his sheep.

Can you imagine Jesus feeling that way about you? He does! And he also feels that way about the people around you who don't yet have a relationship with him.

Every day you encounter people who don't feel the love of a good shepherd.

Every day you encounter people who don't feel the love of a good shepherd. They have real scars and real wounds that seem to be evidence that either God isn't there or he's not as good as everyone seems to think he is. They watch the news. They see the images of war, murder, and unspeakable atrocities. They are dealing with cancer, divorce, broken families, financial ruin—and the pain makes it hard to believe that God loves them. But we know the truth: he does. He loves us so much that he entered our world, became one of us, and gave his own life for us. And he wants us to be sure that they know and feel that love.

They are the One. And this brings us to our passage in Luke 15.

The Value of Lost Things

Let me set the scene for you again. There was a mixed crowd listening to Jesus. The "church people" were there—the Pharisees and teachers of the law. But there also were the non-churched people, those who did not consider themselves religious or close to God. The crowds loved to gather to hear Jesus teach. He was interesting, bold, and kind. Besides, you never knew when that guy might start doing miracles or handing out fish sandwiches! You never knew what was going to happen when Jesus came around.

Jesus spoke about God's love in a way that was different from the religious folks—who were not there to learn from Jesus. They seemed more interested in criticizing him. This group called the Pharisees was even disturbed that Jesus chose to speak to the common people at all! They were obviously sinners, and a large portion of the Pharisees' theology seemed to be "don't hang around with bad people."

Let's read the passage:

> ¹Tax collectors and other notorious sinners often came to listen to Jesus teach. ²This made the Pharisees and teachers of religious law complain that he was associating with such sinful people—even eating with them!
>
> ³So Jesus told them this story: ⁴"If a man has a hundred sheep and one of them gets lost, what will he do? Won't he leave the ninety-nine others

in the wilderness and go to search for the one that is lost until he finds it? ⁵*And when he has found it, he will joyfully carry it home on his shoulders.* ⁶*When he arrives, he will call together his friends and neighbors, saying, 'Rejoice with me because I have found my lost sheep.'* ⁷*In the same way, there is more joy in heaven over one lost sinner who repents and returns to God than over ninety-nine others who are righteous and haven't strayed away!"*

(Luke 15:1-7)

This story emphasizes the shepherd going into the wilderness, a place out of his norm, to track down and rescue the sheep that has gone astray. This is the message Jesus wants everyone in his audience to understand. Every sheep in the flock has value. Those close to him and those who are living far away.

Jesus knew that he had two audiences listening to him in the crowd that day. It wasn't divided between the "sinners and the saints." It was more like "the sinners who knew they were sinners and the sinners who thought they were better than everyone else." So, Jesus told three short stories about lost things with a message to each group.

To the sinners who knew they were sinners: You are the Ones I'm looking for. You are lost and are precious to me. I'm searching for you!

To the religious folks: You are lost and don't know it. Follow me! My mission is to seek and save the lost. Come join me in my mission! Help me find the Ones who are lost.

One of the things we need to realize about being lost is that the very category of "lostness" indicates value. You are valuable to God. Think about a paper clip. You don't really lose a paper clip. You may misplace it, but you don't call your friends on the phone and say, "Quick, come over,

I've lost my paper clip." It doesn't have much value. It can be replaced. We use the term *lost* when something of great value is missing—like a wedding ring.

Our son, Josh, was about eight years old and needed to get out of the house. I decided to take him to the church playground so he could get out some pent-up energy. We packed a little picnic and headed out. All was going great. We ate our snacks, and Josh was having fun. After about an hour, I started packing up. That's when I noticed my wedding ring was missing.

I mentally and physically backtracked to try to remember the last time I had felt it or seen it on my finger. I knew I had it when we left the house. I thought I had it on the playground. I looked in the obvious places first, trying to track Josh's movements—swings, nope; slide, not there; monkey bars, don't see it. Finally, I thought of the trash can. The huge green, industrial playground trash can full of week-old chicken wings and dirty diapers. I had dumped our picnic trash in there earlier. Could it have slipped off then? Unlikely. Maybe. I'm not sure. I'd better check under the swings again—at least there are no dirty diapers there. But it wasn't under the swings or the slide or the monkey bars. Eventually that trash can, as unappealing as it looked, was turning out to be the most logical place to search next.

At first, I tried to make it a game and get Josh to help me. He was a kid, after all, and kids don't mind disgusting stuff, right?

"Hey Josh, new game, buddy. It's called 'Find Daddy's Ring.' Don't eat those old chicken wings, and try not to touch the diaper; but beside that, no rules. I'll turn over the trash can and time you to see how fast you can find it. On your mark, get set…"

But Josh was too smart. It was too gross even for an eight-year-old boy!

So that just left me. I told myself I could do it. And I did. I turned that trash can over with all the old food, dirty diapers, and unidentifiable liquids sloshing around and went through that garbage piece by piece. It felt like looking for a needle in a haystack when you're not even sure if there is a needle in the haystack. Why was I doing this? Because that ring had value. Not just because it was jewelry, but because of what it represented. It was valuable to me. I wanted it. I valued it. It was lost, so I searched for it. And I found it! Somewhere between an apple core and a Styrofoam tray came a glimmer. It was my ring! I literally rejoiced!

There will never be a more noble goal for your life than sharing Christ with those who don't yet know him.

Whom do you know who does not yet have a relationship with Jesus? God loves that person, and he is counting on you to reach out to him or her. There are so many Scriptures that let us know that once we have been found, our primary purpose on earth is to love God and love others. There will never be a more noble goal for your life than sharing Christ with those who don't yet know him. If you need a little motivation, here are a few passages:

> "For God so loved the world that He gave His only begotten Son, that whoever believes in Him should not perish but have everlasting life."
> (John 3:16 NKJV)

> For God made Christ, who never sinned, to be the offering for our sin, so that we could be made right with God through Christ.
> (2 Corinthians 5:21)

²¹You... were once far away from God. You were his enemies, separated from him by your evil thoughts and actions. ²²Yet now he has reconciled you to himself through the death of Christ in his physical body. As a result, he has brought you into his own presence, and you are holy and blameless as you stand before him without a single fault.

(Colossians 1:21-22)

God decided in advance to adopt us into his own family by bringing us to himself through Jesus Christ. This is what he wanted to do, and it gave him great pleasure.

(Ephesians 1:5)

"For God did not send his Son into the world to condemn the world, but to save the world through him."

(John 3:17 NIV)

He gave his life to purchase freedom for everyone. This is the message God gave to the world at just the right time.

(1 Timothy 2:6)

But now in Christ Jesus you who once were far away have been brought near by the blood of Christ.

(Ephesians 2:13 NIV)

"For the Son of Man came to seek and save those who are lost."

(Luke 19:10)

As far as sheep go, I'd say most don't mean to get lost. But they—OK, we—have a tendency to wander away from the flock and away from the Shepherd. Let me ask you again, whom do you know who needs Jesus? Who are you praying for and actively seeking to bring to Christ?

If you are "found," if you know and love Jesus, then set aside your own agenda and get active in the family business. Let's get out there and help find the lost Ones! Here's a prayer to help us get started:

Dear Father,

I want to get involved with your Mission. I'm sorry I've been too busy with my own agenda and busyness. I want to correct that now. Lord, please show me someone I can help today. Let my heart hurt for the "One" person in my life who is lost and that You want me to search for and try to bring to You. I pray this in Jesus's name. Amen.

FOR INSPIRATION

Lee's Story

Childhood for me was interesting. One of my earliest memories is of my dad doing a line of cocaine off of my framed baby picture. There was lots of fighting and no peace in our home. My father was also a cheater. Eventually, Mama took me and my siblings and we moved into project housing. Life was hard, and my dad continued to seek us out and even kidnapped us at one point. A vivid childhood memory is waiting for someone to get us after the police found us.

I hoped my messy childhood was over, but it wasn't.

My mom later remarried. Childhood felt pretty normal for a while, but my mom became more and more emotionally unstable the older we got. She always told us how much she hated teenage girls—and that was me. She smoked a lot, and although I hated the smoking, it calmed her down and was the only time I felt I could approach her.

I tried to fill my life with positive things. I was a good student who made good grades, an athlete, well-liked by my peers and coaches, a class officer, and the list goes on. I tried hard, but things deteriorated with my mother. One day when I was in high school, we had an argument. It was bad. She followed me out of the house, tackled me, and began hitting me. My stepdad rescued me and sent me on to school that day. But when I came home, I was locked out. I never lived at home again. Friends and family took me in, and I tried to make sense of my life.

I lived with friends and extended family and finished high school. College came next, but that was a hard season.

Lots of time being with friends, joining campus groups, and partying led to many poor decisions. I was searching. I made poor decisions sexually. I had a serious boyfriend at one point and got pregnant. I made the decision to do what I never could now. I had an abortion. Easily, it was the worst day of my life.

Talk about a lost sheep—yeah, that was me at this point.

Eventually, I met the love of my life. He really saw me and loved me. We married, but the first years were really hard. We were struggling. My best friend growing up had always encouraged me to seek Jesus. It was always at the back of my mind. Maybe that was our answer?

Then, I had three different friends invite us to church. My son was around one, and we knew we wanted him to have a better foundation in life than we had. We went to church on Easter one year and then went randomly for the next four or five years.

Then one year we decided to try and attend church every Sunday that year after a message from our pastor. We did. I think we only missed a small handful of services that year. We were struggling financially, and I remember in the middle of the night just getting on my knees and crying and praying to God to help us sell this truck that we needed to sell. It sold at full price in just a few days. I knew this was a clear sign that I was headed in the right direction. I knew God was with me. For the first time I could really feel him.

That fall we started serving as ushers at church, and the next year we started tithing. I was eventually asked to lead the usher team and then work part-time at the church. I was a busy mom with two small kids and a job that I loved. How would I have time for that? How could I not? Three months later I was asked to work at the church full-time, and I've been there ever since.

My passion is Jesus and his people. I love people. I know how to make people feel welcome. I empathize with their hurt and celebrate their joy. I really believe that if I can get them through the doors of the church, they will be amazed at how the people in this place are filled with so much joy and love. If getting them here means organizing a friendly greeter team, offering a donut, or creating a huge party, then so be it. I want everyone to feel what I get to wake up and feel every day, which is the calming assurance of unconditional love.

I am so grateful that people loved me enough to obediently invite me to a safe place to meet Jesus. Looking back, the funny thing is that God was always there. He was just waiting for me to reach out to him. Yes, my childhood was rocky at times, but I never really knew that until I got older.

Now, I want to use my story to help others in their journey. God was there for me when I didn't even know how to reach out to him. He's there for you too, if you're hurting.

Now, I know of at least twenty people who attend church regularly after I invited them. They were once my Ones. I will never stop inviting and seeking because God never stops seeking us. I would love to just send a mass text to the world telling them, "Jesus loves you! Seek him!" and have everyone have ears to hear it. How cool would that be?

In Search of the One,

Lee

FOR MEMORIZATION

"The Son of Man came to seek and to save the lost."

(Luke 19:10 NIV)

FOR REFLECTION

- Reread the parable of the lost sheep and imagine yourself as the lost sheep. How do you feel knowing the shepherd left the flock on a search-and-rescue mission just for you?
- What did it feel like to be lost?
- How often do you invite someone to join you in worship? Weekly, monthly, hardly ever, never?
- Whom do you know who is far from God? How can you show that person love this week?
- Who is your One? Begin today to pray for him or her daily.

THE COIN

Luke 15:8-10

JEN

Some of these people have missed the most
important thing in life—they don't know God.
(1 Timothy 6:21 TLB)

Before I traveled to Africa, I received a vaccination for yellow fever for the first time. It pinched for a second but wasn't too bad—at first. Then the symptoms began: low-grade fever, aches, swelling, and pain at the injection site. I had a slight case of yellow fever, and it made me feel terrible. When I called the doctor to inquire, she said, "That makes sense. You were injected with a small amount of the disease so that your body can build up immunity to it. That vaccine will give you a resistance so that you will never develop the real thing." It felt to me like I had the real thing, but I didn't. I had been vaccinated.

Being vaccinated from things we don't want to contract is a good thing. But being vaccinated from things we need in our lives is dangerous. It appears that many people in our churches today are what might be called *vaccinated Christians*. They have been exposed to just enough religion that they believe in Jesus, but they've never developed a real relationship with him. They carry a small "trace of Christianity" within them, but it's not enough to develop the real thing. In other words, they like the idea of being a Christian without truly surrendering their lives to Christ. This accidental immunization is a subtle process that leaves many well-intentioned people far short of the goal of actually following Christ as the Lord of their lives. In fact, they may not know that there is more for them than just the knowledge of God. My fear, and I'm guessing you share it, is that many churches are filled with immunized Christians.

When my son, Josh, was six, he came to me, with a very serious look, and said, "Mom, growing up in the church and in our home, I've learned a lot about Jesus. But I think I just know about him, I'm not sure I really know him. How do I get to know him?" This was a deeply insightful moment for such a little guy. That day began his quest to know Christ for himself, a journey that has been precious to watch. It has been powerful to see his transformation from knowing about Christ to following him faithfully.

We live in a world that suffers from spiritual emptiness.

We live in a world that suffers from spiritual emptiness. In fact, the things of God often feel like foolishness to people in our society. But this is not a new dilemma. In the first century, Paul addressed his apprentice in the faith, Timothy, when he wrote, "For the message of the cross is foolishness to those who are perishing, but to us who are being saved it is the power of God" (1 Corinthians 1:18 NIV). This verse resonates deeply in me. The cross is everything. It is the power of God at work in our lives. It is the hope of a world desperately in need of hope, but to so many it is foolishness. What happened at the cross paved the road for all to have eternal life, but so many have missed that. Does that break your heart? I hope so. Because when our hearts become broken, we often move into action.

Earlier in ministry, I did a great deal of work with students. One afternoon, one of my youth came to see me with tear-filled eyes. A few years earlier she had a life-changing experience with Jesus. Since that time, she had been living for Christ privately and publicly. Her faith was growing. It was obvious that she spent time in prayer and Bible study, and her character matched her testimony. So, it was surprising to find her on my doorstep in tears. As she began to pour out her heartache, I learned that her dad had been making family jokes about her faith. She was considered the fanatical family member who was taking this whole God thing way too seriously. At first I thought she was embarrassed, or maybe even mad, at their teasing. But I was wrong. Her pain was from worry that her family did little more than attend church. She was afraid they had embraced a cultural but not personal understanding of Christ, and it was breaking her heart.

That afternoon we prayed together, and I shared with her the message of 1 Corinthians 1:18 (NIV): "The message of the cross is foolishness to those who are perishing, but to us who are being saved it is the power of God." Her eyes filled again, and she said, "Yes! What they see as foolish in my life is the very power of God I have experienced. How can I help them know the God I love?" Her passion to see her loved ones come to know a deep and fulfilling relationship with Christ left a huge impression on me that day.

First Timothy 6:21 says, "Some of these people have missed the most important thing in life—they don't know

God" (TLB). What a tragedy to live an entire life having missed the most important thing—knowing and loving God. Consider the missed joy, peace, and wisdom while on earth. But, much more important, what about the eternal implications? To miss Jesus is to be separated eternally from him. To miss a real relationship with him is to miss heaven. That's not theoretical, it's biblical fact, and it should motivate us to a deep conviction to spend our lives pursuing those who are lost.

Whether the people in our world suffer as vaccinated Christians or have a view that the things of God are foolishness, our response must be the same. We must seek what is lost. And we must do it with a motivation of love.

The Old Testament contains more than six hundred laws that the people of God tried to keep on a daily basis.[1] It had to be overwhelming at times. So, it's no wonder that in Matthew 22:36 Jesus is essentially asked: "Out of all the laws in the Bible, which is the most important?" It's a good question. His answer is beautifully concise: "'Love the Lord your God with all your heart and with all your soul and with all your mind.' This is the first and greatest commandment. And the second is like it: 'Love your neighbor as yourself.' All the Law and the Prophets hang on these two commandments" (vv. 37-40 NIV).

When questioned, Jesus gets right to the heart of the matter: love. Passionately, diligently, and unashamedly, we are to love God and his people. Now, the other Scriptures are not to be discarded, but Jesus puts into perspective where our focus must be. Love. In fact, his response to this question has become known as the Great Commandment: Love God and love others. It is with this backdrop that we turn to the second parable in Luke 15.

Of Great Value

Luke is a compassionate writer. His Gospel gives great attention to stories of the hurting, the lost, the beggars, the widows, and the needy. In the three famous parables told by Jesus in chapter 15, we see the heart of Christ. There is a passion and deep sense of grief for finding what is lost. We've seen in the first story that the shepherd is not content with a majority, but is diligent to care for the whole of his flock. And then, when found, there is celebration. Real celebration —like Super Bowl, baby announcement, win-the-lottery kind of celebration! If we read Luke 15 and miss the emotions of heartache, passion, and joy, we have missed a great deal!

The second parable Jesus tells while gathered with the crowd involves a woman and her treasure. This story is only a few straightforward verses. A woman loses a coin. She looks for it. And then she's happy when she finds it. It seems simple. But as we explore it today, consider her emotions. She's not just looking for a coin; she is desperately looking for a treasure. This is not a casual search. She tears apart her home to find it. And when it's found, she parties.

Can you remember a time when you, too, were desperate? Try to recall those feelings as you read this famous parable:

> [8]*"Suppose a woman has ten silver coins and loses one. Doesn't she light a lamp, sweep the house and search carefully until she finds it? [9]And when she finds it, she calls her friends and neighbors together and says, 'Rejoice with me; I have found my lost coin.' [10]In the same way, I tell you, there is rejoicing in the presence of the angels of God over one sinner who repents."*
>
> *(Luke 15:8-10 NIV)*

When I was sixteen, I went to the hospital to visit my grandmother. It was the last time I saw her alive. In our visit she took a ring off her finger and placed it on mine. She knew the cancer would soon take her, and she wanted me to have something of hers that she valued. I wore it almost every day. So, a few years later when I noticed it unexpectedly missing from my hand, I panicked. I searched the entire house. My family helped me search. It was a thorough, disconnect-the-pipe-in-the-bathroom-sink kind of search. But we could not find it. (You'll recall that Jim shared about losing a ring in the last chapter. Apparently, we have issues with losing rings!)

Months later, while putting on a sweater, an object dropped to the floor. It was the precious ring. Apparently, it had caught while taking off the sweater the previous winter and had been safely waiting for me to find it the following fall. As I placed it back onto my hand, I dropped to the floor and tearfully thanked God that it was found. They were tears of relief and celebration. That which had been lost was found!

Of course, it was only a ring. And in the parable it is only a coin. But to me, this particular ring had great worth, just as this coin had great value to the woman in the parable. The point of each of these parables in Luke 15 is to teach the religious folks that everyone has worth, even tax collectors and notorious sinners. (By the way, don't you love that the adjective *notorious* is included? These are not your run-of-the-mill sinners!)

Let's consider the value of the coin for a moment. Historians and commentators offer many possibilities about the origin and worth of the lost coin from this parable. Perhaps it was part of a woman's common headdress of the day, where ten coins were strung together and worn on the forehead over the veil. This ornament, often given at the wedding, could be considered the equivalent of a wedding ring today. Some commentaries even speculate that to lose this would be a disgrace to her husband.

Perhaps, the ten coins were her dowry—a symbol from her family given at her wedding to ensure that she is properly cared for. If this were the case, then the coin represents security and has rich history from her family.

Or maybe the coins, each worth about a day's wage, simply signified all of her worldly wealth. In which case, to lose even one coin would be a great loss. Truthfully, it's not imperative that we know the origin and worth of this coin; it's enough to know that for this woman, it had great value. Perhaps to others it would not have seemed worth the effort; others might have thought her foolish. But for her, it was a treasure worth great effort to find.

Like the shepherd in the first story, the odds of loss may seem low to us, 99 to 1 with the sheep and 9 to 1 with the coins. But we see in both of these parables the owners are not content with a majority. Instead, they go to great lengths to restore what is missing. In the telling of these parables, Jesus is stressing to the Pharisees the value of that which they may have overlooked, or simply found not worth seeking, which are the tax collectors and notorious sinners.

What may seem insignificant in the eyes of the world is of great value to [Jesus].

Let's break this down. What is Jesus really communicating here? He is wanting the Pharisees and teachers in the synagogues to see that what may seem insignificant in the eyes of the world is of great value to him. That's what he wants us to understand as well.

At some level, you probably already know that there is not a person you will ever meet, not a single one, whom Jesus did not die for. We already know that to live as true disciples, we must move past the phase of vaccinated Christian and intentionally take on the role of searching for the lost. It's probably not new information to you that God wants every one of his creation to come to know and love him, to be adopted into the family. You most likely already know that he's not content with a majority but desires the whole: all one hundred sheep, all ten coins—and as we will see, both sons. We read in 2 Peter 3:9, "The Lord is not slow in keeping his promise, as some understand slowness. Instead he is patient with you, not wanting **anyone** to perish, but everyone to come to repentance" (NIV, emphasis added).

So, we have to ask ourselves, How does this affect how we live daily? Are we willing to go up steep cliffs and through the thorns like the shepherd for the lost sheep? Do we share this woman's passion to clean the house meticulously for the lost coin? And as we will see in the next chapter, are we willing to throw propriety out the window and run to those in need of Jesus?

In Luke 15, we see that the church leaders had gathered to hear Jesus teach, but they had missed the heart of God. The presence of rough folks offended them. The fact that Jesus was developing intimate relationships with these people troubled them even more. As a parent, I understand this; as my children developed friendships, I wanted their deepest relationships to be with like-minded young people. Kids who loved God, made wise decisions, and treated others with respect were my first choices for their close friendships. But, I also wanted them to be friendly to everyone. In fact, a saying Jim has incorporated around our house and church is "Be friendly first."

The simple act of friendship is such a powerful way to let people, even those living far outside the bounds of God's law, know that they have value. Do these have to be our closest relationships? No, but that doesn't mean they aren't real friendships, nonetheless. As Jesus tells these parables he emphasizes that his love and salvation are for all people— no matter how far from him they may be living.

The simple act of friendship is such a powerful way to let people, even those living far outside the bounds of God's law, know that they have value.

Dream Big

Let's think about some practical applications for this famous chapter 15. Consider, for instance, who the "notorious sinners" of your community might be. Again, we all sin. This is not an attempt to label or divide. What are their stories? How have their lives been challenging? What are their hurts, and how do they perceive the church? Would they be warmly welcomed into your congregation? Are you as a congregation making intentional efforts to invite and serve people living far from God's standards? Do people from various races, socioeconomic situations, and faith backgrounds regularly attend service? What are your statistics when it comes to first-time professions of faith? Is your setting warm and welcoming to those who don't yet know Christ? If not, get busy! (The previous chapter will help you get started.)

When we were first sent to Middle Georgia to start a church, we hired a "coach" or church consultant. One of his first instructions was to begin to pray that the lost would be drawn to our services. But he went a step further and said, "In fact, pray that a real rascal of the community is saved and becomes vocal about what God has done in their life. There is nothing more powerful than the testimony of a radically changed life." We did exactly that; we began to pray that prayer, and sure enough, God answered it. Those who were far from God, some even "notorious sinners," began to come. Our congregation welcomed them, and God began to move. Even today, we are known as the "church that will let anyone attend." It's usually meant as an insult, but we like it!

Now, a church filled with sinners, especially noteworthy ones, will be messy. But, guess what? We're all messy people, and every church is filled with sinners. So, go ahead and embrace them no matter what variety they come in. Love them right where they are and then point them to the truth and holiness found in Christ.

One of the sayings around our church is that we are on mission "Here, Near, and Far." That means we seek to live out the Great Commandment and Great Commission locally, nationally, and globally in intentional ways. This is our modern translation of Acts 1:8, taking the good news into our Jerusalem, Judea, and Samaria, and the ends of the earth.

What would that look like for you? In your personal relationships among your friends, neighbors, family, and coworkers, who needs to find the love, hope, and salvation that comes through Christ alone? What are you doing to partner with the Holy Spirit to help bring them into relationship with Jesus?

At a local and national level, who has not received the message of Christ in compelling ways? Who is being overlooked? Who are we in the church not actively seeking?

And what about at a global level? What can you and your congregation do to partner with those desperately in need of the love of Christ?

It is likely that in order to have the privilege of sharing at any of these levels, you will first need to care for people. Developing real authentic relationships with people is primary to being able to come alongside them to share Jesus. So, consider first how you can demonstrate the love of Christ in practical ways by caring for people, and then you may have the privilege of eventually sharing Christ with them.

As you dream about these possibilities, dream big! Don't give in to roadblocks as they occur (and they will). Instead, pray through them to find the win, because in this case, the win is abundant life here and now and eternal salvation.

Prepare to Rejoice

The woman in the parable goes on a thorough hunt. A typical village home would have a few small openings for windows, or possibly no windows at all. It would be dark as she begins to search. So, she uses expensive oil to light her way as she sweeps every nook and cranny. The cost of the oil was insignificant. She must find what she has lost. I imagine her on hands and knees hoping the light will cast just a shimmer on the lost coin. She sweeps through once and then twice, again and again covering the small familiar ground hoping to see a glimpse of the precious coin. Panic has set in, but then—the coin is found! And she is elated. She doesn't just rejoice privately; she calls together her friends and neighbors to invite them to share in her joy. What was lost has been found!

Almost weekly in our local setting, we have the opportunity to lead people into a first-time decision to follow

Jesus. It is incredible. But if I'm being perfectly honest, I'm not sure that each of those people is getting the rejoicing they deserve. Each life, each time, is so precious to God. I love the verse that tells us that the angels of heaven rejoice (Luke 15:10)!

One of our friends is waiting for a lost son to return to Jesus, and her testimony ends this chapter. We have fasted and prayed with her, and we believe, as she does, that one day her son will come back to Christ. Her story might be your story, or perhaps there is another One in your life that you are burdened to pray for faithfully. And on that day when our prayers are answered, like the woman who finds her coin, we will rejoice. Oh, how we will rejoice!

FOR INSPIRATION

Jill's Story

As a mother of six kids, there have been times when we forgot a kid at school, or home, or even church. Especially when we drove two cars. Being outnumbered is always a challenge, but we wouldn't trade it for the world.

Everywhere we went, counting kids became a part of what I would do. Always in my head would be one, two, three, four, five, and six. OK, they are all safe. When we would load in the car, I would say, "Let's count off," and my children would begin to say the number in which they entered this earth. Oldest to youngest, of course. And when someone was spending the night away or maybe decided to stay home, it would throw me off. Someone is missing. I would have to remind myself that he or she was not missing or lost, just not with us at the time. The safety of my children and knowing they are where they are supposed to be is my top priority.

I have a lot of titles such as boss lady, speaker, wife, mentor, and friend; but to be honest, my most treasured title is mom. When I look at my children, I am overwhelmed at the goodness of God and how blessed I am that they call me Mom. I have always taken pride in the fact that I have consistently taught my children about Jesus and take them to church every time the doors are open. We have served, taught, led, helped, given, and done anything else we felt like God was telling us to do. But, more than anything, I want my children to love and follow Jesus. I want them to have a relationship with him that guides every single part of their lives.

Now, let's back up six years. My children ranged in age from two to seventeen at the time. Life was good. I was serving in the church, working hard, speaking at women's conferences, and doing all I could do to lead people to Jesus. Everywhere I went, I was looking for someone who was lost, someone I could share the love of Christ with; someone I could lead to him. How could I help other people have a home full of believers as I did?

But then one day everything changed. I will never forget standing in my kitchen and the Lord prompting me to ask my oldest son how his relationship with Jesus was going. I could have never prepared myself for the response. He said something like this, "Mom, I really don't know what I believe anymore. I don't really think God is real. If he is real, why would he let babies die or bad things happen? I just don't believe anymore. There can't be a God. I just don't believe." That day everything changed for me. I realized that my sweet boy was lost. He had been wandering and I didn't even know. He had been searching and I didn't even know. He had wandered to a place that was far from Jesus. I had nothing "spiritual" to say in that moment. I had no wisdom, no great Scriptures, nothing. I was devastated. I was confused. I was hurt. I was angry. I was frustrated. My husband and I had never felt grief like this. We didn't sleep well for months. And the more I begged my son to reconsider Jesus, the further he ran. I handled it all wrong. I said stupid things. I begged him to love Jesus. I spent months asking, "Do you believe yet?" I pushed. I quoted. I begged. I cried.

Why me, Lord? I serve you. I love you. I give you my everything. Why am I having to go through this? Why is my son lost? My sweet boy. I taught him about you. I took him to church. I taught him to serve you. Crying was normal at this point. Desperation was an understatement. What if something happened to him? What if? What if? What if?

Then it hit me, Am I going to sit around and worry about me, or am I going to fight with everything I have for the salvation of my son? Am I going to do my part and trust God with the rest? Am I going to believe that there is someone who actually loves my children more than me? Jesus does. He actually gently put that in my spirit one day. "Don't you know that I love him more than you?" Well then, God, what is my part?

Years had gone by with me doing all the wrong things. Desperately I was trying to save my sweet boy myself. Trying to "find" him all by myself. Doing it my way. Then, as I was digging in my Bible one day, I was reminded that some things only come by prayer and fasting. So, I made up my mind that I would never give up. I would do my part and let God do his. I would begin to pray, fast, and love my son. I could not change him. Only God could. So my journey began anew.

In the last six years I have fasted and prayed so much. I have stood and believed. I have hoped as I sat in church that this would be the Sunday he would choose Jesus. I have dealt with frustration, impatience, jealousy, anger, depression, anxiety, and a lot of other feelings throughout this journey. But when those feelings come, I don't stay there. I begin to remind myself that it is not me who finds my son, but the One who created him. I will do my part and God will do his. He knows my son's heart more than anyone else. I begin to pray. I stand firm in the search for my lost son. I stand firm knowing that although I don't yet see him found, I am to continue to pray and fast as my God brings him to the light. I am to stand and know that giving up on him is not an option. I stand and know that one day his testimony of how God never gave up on him will reach thousands.

And every tear, every sleepless night, every day without meat or sweets, every day on my knees with my heart surrendered to a God who knows and sees everything will be worth it! My son is worth it. He is worth every second, every minute, every hour, every day, every year. I will not give up on him. He is worth it.

Praying for my One,

Jill

FOR MEMORIZATION

"For where your treasure is, there your heart will be also."

(Matthew 6:21 NIV)

FOR REFLECTION

- What people groups in your community, nation, and the world do you and your church need to be reaching out to as the family of God?
- Consider your circles of influence: family, extended family, friends, coworkers, neighbors, recreational groups. Where do you have the most influence?
- Who in each of your circles needs to be among your Ones?
- Are you ready to commit to praying for them the way that Jill is praying for her son? Why or why not?

THE BOYS

Luke 15:11-32

JIM

[Jesus] said to them, "Go into all the world and preach the gospel to all creation."

(Mark 16:15 NIV)

The first two parables in Luke 15, the sheep and the coin, are very short, only a few sentences. But the story of the two brothers is longer and more complicated. I suppose that makes sense because sheep and coins are pretty simple and straightforward. But people, well, people are another matter. People are messy. We're complex, complicated. That's just real life.

Have you ever just asked a simple question, expecting a yes or no answer, only to be told, "Well, it's complicated." You want to yell, "Just give me a yes or no!" We've all been there. Sometimes, life is just complicated.

Actually, we've all probably been on both sides of that predicament. We want to give a simple answer. We wish we could tie all the details up in a neat package, but, like I said, it's complicated.

Who is your One? When we ask this question, it really would be simpler if we were searching for a lost animal or a lost piece of jewelry. But when we ask this question, we're asking about people. Who is the One person in your life whom you are going to do your best to seek out and find in order to lead him or her to Jesus? Who is the One whom God is leading you to pursue in order to lead him or her toward him? Our hearts hurt for the One until he or she is found.

This is important to remember: lost people don't want to be our little projects.

I hope you are praying for your One, engaging with that person in conversation, and listening for his or her hurts. But as you ease into the family business of seeking and saving the lost (Luke 19:10), let me reiterate a little warning that we shared earlier. I don't want to dampen your enthusiasm, but this is important to remember: lost people don't want to be our little projects. And oftentimes, lost people aren't really interested in being found. It's complicated. I get the little project thing. I've been on the receiving end of that kind of attention, and I did not like it.

When I was in college, my good buddy (who had a girl-friend at the time) decided to set me up on a blind date—a blind, double date with him and his girlfriend, to be exact. His girlfriend had this friend, so they thought it would be fun to get us together and we'd all hit it off and have fun. Sounds reasonable so far, right? Well, my friend's girlfriend was pretty cute, so I thought her friend might be cute too. I was game.

Now, you have to realize, I'm from a small town (think Mayberry), so the entertainment options were limited. That explains the excitement my buddy and I felt when we heard the Royal Lipizzaner Stallions were coming to town! If you aren't familiar with them, these are famous white horses from Austria. I love horses, so this sounded awesome!

OK, I know you're laughing at me right now. I'll give you a second to get your composure.

I'll admit that maybe this was not the most appropriate venue for a blind date. But remember, our choices were limited.

At any rate, I was as excited about seeing the horses as I was about the date. Things went well at first. Introductions were made. We were four college students trying to grow up, follow Jesus, and have fun. It was even put forth that I was thinking about becoming a pastor, which by the way, is a kind of dating litmus test for some girls. In my experience, this information about vocational ministry seemed to promote extreme but opposite reactions from single females. As a teenager, when I would mention to a prospective date that I was going into ministry, she either ran for the hills to escape or started picking out wedding china. I was shocked by both reactions because, at that time, I just wanted to hang out and share a pizza. As it turns out, my blind date fell into the second category; she liked the idea of being a pastor's wife.

On the other hand, I was really just interested in eating some pizza and watching some cool horses.

As I said, things went well at first. We took the girls out to eat before the show. Conversation was light and casual. And then it happened. Suddenly the conversation turned to our faith, and through our discussion the girls discovered that, according to them, I had the wrong kind of faith—meaning, I was from a different denomination than they were. The questions and probes toward me became more intense, to the level of theological debate on their part. I wasn't interested in debating. In fact, very quickly I wasn't interested in being in the same zip code as these two young ladies anymore. How did this date turn into the Spanish Inquisition?

Several things intensified during that long, long night.

First, the girls kept turning up the heat. Evidently, they thought I was still a good catch if I could be turned from the Dark Side (which was my particular denomination). These girls seemed to be under the impression that if you weren't a part of their denomination, and maybe if you weren't a member of their particular church, you were on a slippery slope to H-E-Double Hockey Sticks. I became their little project. What a trophy of their zeal I would be if I'd just join their denomination and their church.

The second thing that happened was my friend kept mouthing "I'm sorry, I'm so sorry" throughout that long, dark night of the soul.

The last thing that happened is that I tuned out listening to the girls entirely. Instead, I plotted and schemed how to get back at my friend for this horrendous experience. I'm still working on that one!

That was over thirty years ago. My buddy and I are still good friends, and yes, I still enjoy giving him a hard time about that blind date whenever I can. I don't know what happened to the girls. I'm sure they were well-intentioned. We were young, and in our youth we often make mistakes. I hope they found some nice boys whose faith background aligned with theirs and are living happily ever after.

But here's the lesson I learned that night, and it's one I hope I'll never forget: No one wants to be your little project. No one wants you to try to save them if you aren't willing to really listen and care about them first. It feels icky and insincere. It feels fake and artificial. It feels like the person trying to convert or save you doesn't really care about you at all.

It often makes you feel as if you are a part of an agenda, a notch on a belt, or a check mark on a self-righteous to-do list. It doesn't feel good. First and foremost people need to know that you truly care.

As we begin to engage or reengage in a fresh way with Jesus's mission to seek and save the lost, we need to remember that the how matters. How we seek people, how we listen, how we engage and invite can make all the difference. We can do the right thing (trying to connect people to Jesus) in the wrong way (treating people as a project) and mess up the whole thing.

> ### *How we seek people, how we listen, how we engage and invite can make all the difference.*

Jesus loved the people he met. He was genuinely warm and friendly. People wanted to be around him.

I've heard Christians say that their churches are small, or that they don't have many friends, because they stand for the "real gospel." Sometimes they even claim that larger churches or ministries got that way by being watered down or disingenuous to Christ. Maybe that's true in some cases. But I would say that sometimes our churches are small and we don't have many friends because we aren't very nice. People like to be around other people who treat us with dignity and respect. We avoid people who come across as judgmental or superior.

An attitude of superiority was part of the Pharisees' problem in Luke 15. They were convinced that they were better than those in the crowd, and that attitude showed when they interacted with people outside their religious context. So, don't be discouraged about helping your One. Get past faith-sharing formulas and techniques. Be yourself. Be genuinely interested and caring for other people. Compassion is key when it comes to sharing the love of Jesus.

Two Lost Boys—Hollywood Style

This brings us to the third story in Luke 15, a story about two lost boys. As you know, there is an assortment of people in the crowd as Jesus begins the story.

> [11]"There was a man who had two sons. [12]The younger one said to his father, 'Father, give me my share of the estate.' So he divided his property between them.
>
> [13]"Not long after that, the younger son got together all he had, set off for a distant country and there squandered his wealth in wild living. [14]After he had spent everything, there was a severe famine in that whole country, and he began to be in need. [15]So he went and hired himself out to a citizen of that country, who sent him to his fields to feed pigs. [16]He longed to fill his stomach with the pods that the pigs were eating, but no one gave him anything.
>
> [17]"When he came to his senses, he said, 'How many of my father's hired servants have food to spare, and here I am starving to death! [18]I will set out and go back to my father and say to him: Father, I have sinned against heaven and against you. [19]I am no longer worthy to be called your son; make me like one of your hired servants.'

²⁰*So he got up and went to his father.*

"But while he was still a long way off, his father saw him and was filled with compassion for him; he ran to his son, threw his arms around him and kissed him.

²¹*"The son said to him, 'Father, I have sinned against heaven and against you. I am no longer worthy to be called your son.'*

²²*"But the father said to his servants, 'Quick! Bring the best robe and put it on him. Put a ring on his finger and sandals on his feet.* ²³*Bring the fattened calf and kill it. Let's have a feast and celebrate.* ²⁴*For this son of mine was dead and is alive again; he was lost and is found.' So they began to celebrate.*

²⁵*"Meanwhile, the older son was in the field. When he came near the house, he heard music and dancing.* ²⁶*So he called one of the servants and asked him what was going on.* ²⁷*'Your brother has come,' he replied, 'and your father has killed the fattened calf because he has him back safe and sound.'*

²⁸*"The older brother became angry and refused to go in. So his father went out and pleaded with him.* ²⁹*But he answered his father, 'Look! All these years I've been slaving for you and never disobeyed your orders. Yet you never gave me even a young goat so I could celebrate with my friends.* ³⁰*But when this son of yours who has squandered your property with prostitutes comes home, you kill the fattened calf for him!'*

> ³¹*"'My son,' the father said, 'you are always with me, and everything I have is yours.* ³²*But we had to celebrate and be glad, because this brother of yours was dead and is alive again; he was lost and is found.'"*
>
> *(Luke 15:11-32 NIV)*

If you grew up in church, you've probably heard a lot of sermons from this passage of Scripture. My brother-in-law jokes that he has heard this story preached from every perspective possible. He claims the only unexplored territory that remains is the backstory of the fattened calf! When something is that familiar, it can lose the shock and awe that probably was the reaction of the original listeners.

So, to help us look at this parable in a new way, I invite you to use your imagination. Jen and I like going to the movies, so imagine this story as the hottest blockbuster movie coming out of Hollywood. The previews have America clamoring to go to the theaters. All the things that make a movie great are tantalizing us in the previews—action, drama, the rise and fall of the underdog, fortunes gained and lost, romance.

Here's the all-star cast:

Chris Hemsworth (from *Thor*) . . . . Prodigal Son
Robert Downey, Jr. (think *Iron Man*) . . Older Brother
Anthony Hopkins . . . . Father
Various *X-Men* bad guys . . . . Pharisees
Ian McKellen (Magneto from *X-Men*) . Chief Pharisee
Cast from *Braveheart* . . . . "Notorious Sinners"
Special guest star. . . . . . .Josh Gad (Olaf from *Frozen*)
as the voice of the Fattened Calf

That's a cast people would show up to see. Here's the opening scene:

As the camera pans in, Jesus looks around at his crowd—his two crowds, really. Mel Gibson and the *Braveheart* "notorious sinners" are milling around in a raucous mob, bursting into loud laughter as some of their number occasionally moon the Pharisees. Magneto and the rest of the bad *X-Men* Pharisees scoff and look down their noses at the common rabble, occasionally lifting a perfumed handkerchief to their noses to let the crowds know even their aroma is offensive.

What kind of story can get through to these two audiences? Jesus sighs, looks toward heaven for reassurance, and begins. The scene opens with the younger son working in the fields. He is hot, tired, and restless. He takes off his sweat-drenched shirt, knowing the women in the audience will gasp at his abs. "There's got to be more to life than this one-calf town," he mutters to himself. In frustration, he leaves his older brother working there and goes to find his father.

The younger son says, "Dad, I want what's coming to me. Give me my inheritance now so I can get out of this hick town. I want to find out what the big city is like. I need to find out who I am."

Anthony Hopkins, the dad, is heartbroken. It sounds to him like his son is saying, "I'm tired of waiting around for you to die. Give me the money." After debate, pleas, and tears, Dad finally gives in. "I suppose I can't make you love me, Son, but I'll always love you." The younger son mutters something, hurriedly packs his bags, and heads immediately to the ancient Near Eastern version of Las Vegas, Sin City.

For a while, the son lives out his dream. Vegas and the big world are everything he hoped they would be and more. He finds that with a steady flow of cash, alcohol, and parties, friends are easy to find. Nights are long, filled with "wild living," and most days are spent in a drunken stupor, preparing for a repeat of the night before. He and his parties soon gain a reputation in town as the place to be. His guest list includes the who's who of pop stardom. Anyone who is someone is either in attendance or trying to get in. The rich and famous clamor for an invitation because you never know what might happen at these parties! The local paparazzi follow the son around to see who he's with and what he will do next. He is literally the talk of the town. For a while.

But Vegas is an expensive city, and as his money dries up, so do his friends. Every so-called friend he made at his extravagant soirées now avoids him. Not long ago they laughed at every corny joke he told, but now they laugh at him behind his back. His fancy clothes, toys, and women have all gone away.

To complicate matters further, the economy has taken a downturn due to a famine in the region. The stock market has crashed, and everyone is hurting. At first, he tries to borrow money from some of the connections he has made. But they won't take his messages. As his desperation grows, he tries to get just basic food and shelter from his one-time friends, but now he is just a loser and an embarrassment to them. In desperation, he finds a job at a pig farm outside of town. How did it come to this—a Jewish boy working with unclean pigs? If his family and village could see him now, they would be ashamed.

The work hardly pays anything at all, and he finds himself more hungry, lonely, and lost every day. One day as he's feeding the pigs, he wonders if he can eat their food. After all, pig food is better than starving to death, right?

And that's when it hits him. Everyone's "rock bottom" is different, but this is when and where the son finds his. "What am I doing here? Who am I? The people back home who really loved me, I despised. And the friends I rented now despise me." In a moment of clarity, he devises a plan. "OK, if I stay here, I'll die with these pigs. I've got to go home. I know I can never be a son again, but maybe Dad will give me a job. At least then I won't die." All his pride and arrogance have been burned away. He's desperate.

So he begins the long journey home. He left home on the finest racing camel money could buy, but that was sold off long ago to cover some of the enormous debts he accumulated. Now he has to walk the long, lonely miles. On the return trip, he dreads the first contact with his dad. But he can't think of any other options. So, he practices a speech during the long trek back home. "Dad, I'm sorry. I know I can never make this up to you and never be your son again, but I'm starving, Dad, and I don't know where else to go. Will you give me a job—any job in the business—just so I won't die? I know I don't deserve your help, Sir. I guess I can't even call you 'Dad' anymore, but will you please help me?"

As he walks, he practices his speech over and over. How will he be received? Will he be received at all? Does he even have the right to ask for help? Finally, after his long journey, he begins to recognize landmarks. He's getting closer to home. He fluctuates between hope and despair as he gets closer and closer to home and the father he abandoned. He left as an arrogant rascal, but he's returning in shame, starving.

He knows these roads well. Normally, he would take the next path on the left, but that goes through the village, his village—at least the village that once was his. He can't go through there now. He has to bypass that little hamlet, creep around it, because if he's seen, that will ruin everything. He needs to get to his father first, before the villagers see him; at least then he'll have a chance.

A term passes through his mind that brings with it a shudder—*Kezazah*. It means to be cut off, cast out, excommunicated, shunned, and disowned. It is an ancient tradition of his people.[1] Respect and honor are foundations for his culture and faith. In fact, very unlike today, his culture and faith are so intermingled that there is no separation. He is a Jew both as a nationality and as a religion. He is a son of Abraham, which means he is a member of the Tribe, a part of the covenant people with God himself. Only now, he has broken that covenant. He has dishonored his father, his village, his tribe, his nation, and his God.

The *Kezazah* is a ceremony used by a community to exile someone who has brought shame to their family and hometown.[2] The elders of the village gather around the offender and break a pot at his feet—break it so completely that it cannot be repaired. This symbolizes what the offender has done by breaking covenant with his people. But it also symbolizes the attitude of the community toward the offender. "We break with you. You are cut off. You are broken beyond repair, and you are worse than dead to us. It will be as if you were never born. We will not speak of you. We will not think of you. We will not mourn for you. You are no more."

He knows that this may be his reception. When he left home in the way he did, he not only brought dishonor to his father and family but also disgraced his village and his religion as well. He is an outcast. Returning home as a member of the family would not be tolerated.

So, he skirts the village, staying off the main roads and cutting across plowed fields, to carefully make his way to his father's estate, the place he once called home. That seems like a lifetime ago, and in a way, it was.

He stops. Over the next ridge, he should be able to see his house. He composes himself, now doubting his plan to return. "Well, I've come too far to turn back now." So with the weight of guilt and shame dragging at his feet, he takes the final steps toward home.

He clears the ridge and begins to walk the worn path to his house. Everything looks familiar and different at the same time. He can see the house on the hill, but it's still too far to see if there are people about. Who will be the first to spot him? A servant? What will he or she tell his dad, "A homeless beggar is coming toward the house. Should I run him off?"

Closer now, but still he sees no one in sight. He dreads the moment he will be recognized because that will be the telling time. Will I even be allowed to speak, or will I be driven away? Will the villagers be called? Will my father listen to my speech—oh yeah, my speech. I need to go over it again! He panics for a second because he can't remember his introduction. Oh yeah, "Father, I don't deserve to be your son…" Strong words, but true.

Before he can practice anymore, he sees movement at the house. He has been spotted. It's happening. No turning back. These next moments will decide his future. Someone is running toward him now. He can't make out who it is. Does the person carry a weapon? It doesn't look like he's armed. The son can't tell if it's a good run or a bad run, but the figure is getting closer. The next few seconds baffle the young prodigal. He sees something he has never seen before: his father is…running. That was something his father never did. (In Jesus's culture, people got enough exercise by walking everywhere, so jogging recreationally wasn't a thing. And it was undignified to run. Stately men of importance dressed in dignified robes just didn't run.)

But that's what he's seeing, unless the hunger and long miles are playing tricks on his eyes. He rubs them and looks again. Yes, that's definitely his dad, and he's definitely running—and at an impressive pace too! In seconds his dad has closed the gap and is just yards away.

The son stammers as he tries to begin his speech. "Fa-Father, I've sinned against God and you. I'm not worthy to be your son anymore, but..." Then, to his surprise, his dad leaps for him and wraps him in a strong embrace. The momentum nearly topples them both, but they recover. No words are exchanged for seconds, which seem like hours. Oxygen is becoming a concern because the father's grip makes it difficult to breathe. What is happening right now? Is this an attack?

But it's not. It's the opposite. It's a massive embrace borne out of months of heartache and desperation from a father who thought his wayward son was dead. The son can't see his father's face because the embrace is too tight. He can't tell what emotions rest in his eyes. He can only stand still as his father gasps for breath to speak.

The son flinches in surprise as his father gathers his breath and lets out a roar—an explosive mixture of joy and relief. "My son! My son! You are alive and have returned to me!" The son considers beginning his speech again, but before he can start, his father resumes his shouting. "Bring the best robe and put it on my son. Put a ring on his finger and sandals on his feet. Prepare a feast! Steaks tonight!"

He directs these instructions to the workers scattered around the estate. Some saw the boss running an impressive 100-meter dash and are still standing there gawking with their mouths open in disbelief.

Finally, his father looks him in the eyes, and the son sees a depth of compassion and love that he never dreamed possible. Maybe it was always there and he just missed it all those years. The silence is long but not awkward as his father drinks him in. The son does not shrink from his father's gaze because it is filled with so much joy and love and laughter. But after a while he thinks he should say something. He's about to resume his unfinished speech for the third time when his father begins shouting again, this time to the village and the world and beyond.

"There will be no pots broken today!" he roars. There is a righteous rage in his father's voice this time, but the rage is not directed toward him. It's directed toward anyone who would dare try to harm his son. It's a defiance. A challenge. A warning. The father's eyes flash with fire, and for a fleeting second, the little businessman, his father, is transformed into a warrior. This man is a bear who will gladly fight to the death for his cub.

"This is my son…my son!" he shouts again. Then softer, "My son who was dead has come home."

The next few hours are a blur. The son washes and puts on new clothes. He can't remember the last time he felt clean. A band plays festive music. People laugh and dance and sing. The steaks are cooking on an open fire. Laughter and music and food flow together. It's a party. For just a moment, the son reflects on the irony of it all. He was once the self-proclaimed king of parties, but this one is very different from the raucous galas he hosted while away. This one is more real somehow. It has purpose and meaning.

His gaze scans the room. So many people laughing, celebrating—genuinely excited that he has returned home. He catches his dad's eye from across the room and smiles. A messenger approaches his father and whispers something to him. His dad motions for his son to stay there, then follows the messenger outside.

Outside, Robert Downey, Jr., the older brother, finally has his first speaking part in the movie.

His words are biting, bitter, and angry. "I know what's happened, Dad; the servants told me. How dare he come back like this! And how dare you welcome him this way! All these years I've stayed here and worked with you. I've been faithful and loyal to you. But this son of yours takes your money and blows a fortune on parties and prostitutes, and now you welcome him home with open arms! He doesn't deserve this. I don't deserve this."

"Oh, my son," the father begins sympathetically, "don't you know how much I love you? You have been faithful and loyal all these years, and everything I have is yours. But my dear son, your brother was dead to us, and now he is alive again! He was lost, and now he is found! We have to celebrate his return. Please come in with me and join the celebration."

And suddenly the stage goes dark. The story is abruptly over, and the camera pans in to where it began. Jesus is speaking to one crowd separated into two distinct groups, groups that are visibly hostile to each other. Jesus has taken his audience on a roller-coaster ride of emotions as the hearers begin to recognize themselves in the story.

The *Braveheart* crowd recognizes early on that they are the younger brother. They identify with his rebellious attitude and disregard for anything other than selfish living. No one is surprised when the younger son comes to the end of his resources and is facing tough circumstances. The Pharisees snicker, thinking, *That's what you get!*

But both sides gasp in surprise at the homecoming. No one expected this! Suddenly the story takes an amazing twist. The younger son does not get what he deserves. Instead, he gets what he doesn't deserve: forgiveness, mercy, and restoration. The *Braveheart* crowd bursts into laughter and applause at this. It's not the sarcastic, rowdy laughter from earlier that day. It's a laughter filled with hope.

They are surprised to hear that the father runs! And if the father in the story is God and they are the younger boy, then God is running to *them*! This is new. After all, most of God's spokespersons were these pompous Pharisees who looked down on them with judgment and condescension. They had concluded that God must be like that too. But, what if that isn't the case. What if God *did* run? Is that possible? Would he run to them? If that's true, then this man Jesus has turned their worldview upside down.

Sometime during the story, the Pharisees begin to realize that this parable is about them too. They are the older brother. Precise, strict, and loyal. But also legalistic, condescending, and judgmental toward others. Their snide remarks about the younger brother subside as the story continues and they realize that Jesus is not painting them in a good light. The religious crowd feels discomfort from Jesus's gaze as he tells the story. Some become angry. "We are the chosen ones! We are the faithful! No one keeps the Law as well as we do. Surely God loves us and despises them, as we do." Anger turns to hatred for some, and these religious leaders literally want this upstart preacher dead. "Who does he think he is anyway? Trying to teach us. We are the Pharisees!" But others in the religious crowd listen more closely, pondering and questioning their own image of God as a stern, nearly unpleasant deity compared to the running father God in Jesus's story. Could he be right?

They realize this story is not about a lost boy; it's about two lost boys. One is lost in a faraway land. The other is lost at home. One is wild, rowdy, and lost. The other is quiet, cynical, and lost. One is far from God because of selfish desires. The other is far from God because of selfish hypocrisy.

In the final scene of our movie, we see Jesus conclude his story and look both crowds in the eyes. The invitation has been given: "Come home." As the camera fades, no one has closure because the questions hang in the air on several levels:

- Will the older brother come into the house with the father?
- Will the Pharisees follow Jesus?
- Will the notorious sinners come home to God?

Then the screen is dark and suddenly silent. The movie has concluded abruptly.

In the audience, some are weeping, some are angry, some are thoughtful. Because the audience is left with the same question: Wherever you are, whichever son you relate to, will you come home?

Tag, You're It

Who do you relate to in the story? Of course, most of our attention is directed at the two lost brothers. If you relate to one of them, then the message, the invitation, is to come home. As we have seen, they are lost in very different ways. People can be lost a thousand miles away, but they can also be lost sitting on a velvety cushioned pew.

This story has a lot to teach us. It is a message for all to "come home," but it is also a mandate to "go get them." Remember our little saying "Found People Find People"? Once we come home, we join the Father's family business, running to the lost. Jesus helps us see a new, more accurate image of God—a God who does something many would consider undignified: he runs to those he loves!

God is filled with compassion and mercy, and his heart aches for those who are lost. So he runs to us, and then, when we are found, he issues an invitation: *Come run with me!*

Remember, no one wants to be your little project, but people do want genuineness, transparency, and authenticity. If you know Jesus, then you have something others need. There are people around you—friends, family, and people you will pass on the street today—who are lost. Some are engaged in wild living and haven't been to church in years, if ever. Many of them believe that God does not love or care for them because they haven't experienced love from the ones who represent him on earth, the church people. They haven't yet experienced the love of the God who runs.

We need to show them. We need to imitate and grow more like the father who ran with passion. He ran with real love for the lost.

What keeps us from this? I suppose a lot of things can: sin, selfishness, self-righteousness, or complacency. Or maybe we don't really know if we should be seeking those messy people, those notorious sinner types. The Pharisees struggled with this. It was hard for them to imagine that God would seek, even run toward, people caught in sin. This is a common struggle for us today too.

Loving and accepting people right where they are is what we're called to do.

As you seek to reach the Ones in your life, remember that there is a huge difference between acceptance and approval. You can love, seek, and run to very messy people without putting a stamp of approval on their sinful behaviors. Loving and accepting people right where they are is what we're called to do. I often tell our congregation, "Everyone is welcome—we will love you right where you are. But we will love you deeply enough to tell you the truth from God's Word."

One of the first Scriptures we taught our children was, "Walk with the wise and become wise, / for a companion of fools suffers harm" (Proverbs 13:20 NIV). It's important because you become like those you hang around.

But, friend, there comes a time when we need to grow up in our faith, a time when we reach a level of spiritual maturity so that we are not afraid, offended, or influenced by people far from God. We need to reach a place where we can help pull others up without letting them pull us under.

Here's the thing: we can accept people without approving of what they are doing. This has been a big lesson for us. The father didn't approve of his prodigal son's behavior. He did not give a stamp of approval for his sins, but he did accept him when he came home.

When the woman caught in adultery was thrown at Jesus's feet for judgment, he showed acceptance for her as a person in need of God without approving or endorsing her lifestyle and choices (John 8:3-11). He tells her two sweet things (allow me to paraphrase here):

1. I don't condemn you; you are loved.
2. Stop doing the things you were doing; go and sin no more.

Without grace, we can become snobbish and condemning. Without truth, there are no absolutes, no right or wrong.

This is grace and truth. Without grace, we can become snobbish and condemning. Without truth, there are no absolutes, no right or wrong. In accepting people, we offer both grace and truth in large measures but do not approve or condone sinful behaviors.

Like everything else, this takes practice. We need to practice it individually and corporately as the church. When we first started our church, we said lightheartedly that we are "building a church for people who don't go to church," and that's kind of like building a steak house for vegetarians. That makes a cute little phrase, but we really didn't know what it would mean for us. It meant that we had to learn to invite and welcome "messy" people into the church. Our image of church had to change from a "fortress of the saints" to be more like an "ER for the injured." Actually, you have to be both at the same time, teaching the saints how to love and accept messy, hurting, lost people while not condoning actions or lifestyles that contradict God's Word. It means welcoming people who know they are lost *and* those who don't.

I hope the church you attend is warm and welcoming to folks who are far from God. If it's not, maybe *you* can be the thermostat that will help change the temperature and atmosphere there.

When I was a kid, one of my favorite games was the classic Hide-and-Go-Seek. Surely, you have played this at some point in your life. There are different variations, so let me describe my favorite version for you. Of course, there is one person who is It. The Seeker. Everyone else is a Hider. You remember how the game starts. It starts by the Seeker counting down from an agreed-upon number while the rest of the group, the Hiders, scatter looking for cover. When the countdown concludes, It shouts out those familiar words, "Ready or not, here I come!" Then It goes to work seeking the Hiders.

That's the standard operating procedure for most Hide-and-Go-Seek games around the world. But here's the variation I loved as a kid. When the Seeker finds the first person, that person becomes a Seeker too. Because they've been found, they change from Hider to Seeker. Now there are two Seekers searching, seeking, and finding. When the next person is found, he or she also becomes a Seeker. And so it goes. With each person found, a new Seeker is born, and the game continues until the last person is found.

You see where I'm going here, right?

If you know and love Jesus, then tag, you're It! You and I have the wonderful assignment of joining Jesus in being a Seeker until the last One is found.

A sheep, a coin, and two boys—all are lost and all are worth finding. Our world is filled with people who have yet to come to know and understand the love and salvation that comes through Christ. So Jesus invites us to partner with him in doing just that. Go get your One.

FOR INSPIRATION

Bobby's Story

I was born and raised in quite rough circumstances. My dad split when I was young, and my mom was emotionally unavailable. So, I turned to the streets for the love that I thought I was missing. I grew up in gangs, and through my dirty deeds I gained what I thought was respect only to quickly realize that it wasn't love at all. I ended up doing a lot of bad things, knowing on the inside that this wasn't who I was called to be.

My dad was a police officer, and I wanted to be the complete opposite. I got in a lot of trouble. The good thing, though, about his being a police officer was that when things got rough, his influence was helpful. We lived in the same city, but the only time I saw him was when I got in trouble. Every time I got the handcuffs slapped on me, they called my dad. He would take me home, but the guys I ran with would go to jail. Needless to say, that didn't go over well with my gang. In fact, they thought I was snitching. This was a very low time for me. I was looking so hard for love and acceptance.

It didn't occur to me at the time, but God was looking out for me during those dark years. Even in my mess, God had a hedge of protection around me. He even protected me from myself.

After a while, my dad stopped taking me home when I got in trouble, and I would spend time in jail. But even then, God was with me. One miracle after another kept happening to keep me protected, but I wasn't paying attention to what God was doing. Still, God was faithful.

When I was sixteen years old, I got into a fight and was stabbed. When I noticed the sharp pain, I ran and all of a sudden I saw this huge bright light and instantly fell unconscious. By the grace of God, when I woke up I was able to get away. But my injuries were severe. It took a lot, but I was slowly coming to my senses.

In an attempt to get my life on track, I joined the military. As my life came together I felt the continuous draw of God's Spirit. Finally, I gave up my will for God's, and in the desert while in military training, I gave my life to Jesus. After all I had done, all of my running and rebellion, I surrendered to him. I'm so grateful to be chosen by God, forgiven, and loved. Like the younger son in the parable, a lot of my life was spent in rebellion, but God did not give up on me. The church has welcomed me. In no way do I deserve that kind of love and forgiveness, but how grateful I am for it.

A prodigal who came home,

Bobby

FOR MEMORIZATION

We love because he first loved us.
(1 John 4:19 NIV)

For Reflection

- Consider your life. Have you lived more as the older or younger son—or daughter? Why?
- Has anyone ever "run" to you in a dark time? How did that love and attention feel?
- How can you begin to lavish love on those around you—both the older and younger sons (and daughters) in your midst?
- How often do you share your faith with others? What fears keep you from doing this more often?
- What steps can you take to become more like the Father—someone who runs to the lost?
- How can you begin to live as the Father instead of as a lost son—or daughter?
- Whom has God laid on your heart as you read these chapters? How might you seek to reach that person?
- As you reflect on the three parables of Luke 15, what do you sense Jesus calling you to do?

NOTES

Introduction
1. D. T. Niles, *That They May Have Life* (New York: Harper & Brothers, 1951), 96.

Chapter Three
1. "The Law: All 613 Commandments!" https://www.gospeloutreach .net/613laws.html. Accessed April 28, 2021.

Chapter Four
1. Living Bible Verses, s.v. "kezazah," https://sites.google.com/site /livingbibleverses/ke. Accessed April 28, 2021.
2. Object lesson: "Kezazah ceremony"—the prodigal son, Creative Kidswork, www.creativekidswork.com/prayer/142-101-the-kezazah -ceremony-sunday-school-children-ministry-ideas. Accessed April 28, 2021.

Made in United States
North Haven, CT
11 January 2024

47307687R00055